HAL•LEONARD
HARMONICA
PLAY•ALONG

BLUES Classics

CONTENTS

Page	Title	Demo Track	Play-Along Track
2	Baby, Scratch My Back SLIM HARPO	1	2
8	Eyesight to the Blind SONNY BOY WILLIAMSON II	3	4
14	Good Morning Little Schoolgirl SONNY BOY WILLIAMSON I	5	6
21	Honest I Do JIMMY REED	7	8
24	I'm Your Hoochie Coochie Man MUDDY WATERS	9	10
28	My Babe LITTLE WALTER	11	12
34	Ride and Roll SONNY TERRY	13	14
43	Sweet Home Chicago JUNIOR PARKER	15	16
47	HARMONICA NOTATION LEGEND		

Harmonica by Steve Cohen
Guitar by Mike DeRose
Bass, Keyboard, and Drums by Chris Kringel
Keyboard by Kurt Cowling

ISBN 978-1-4234-2614-1

For all works contained herein:
Unauthorized copying, arranging, adapting, recording, Internet posting,
public performance, or other distribution of the printed or recorded
music in this publication is an infringement of copyright.
Infringers are liable under the law.

Visit Hal Leonard Online at
www.halleonard.com

HAL•LEONARD®
CORPORATION
7777 W. BLUEMOUND RD. P.O. BOX 13819
MILWAUKEE, WISCONSIN 53213

Baby, Scratch My Back

By James Moore

H A R M O N I C A
Player: Slim Harpo
Harp Key: B♭ Diatonic

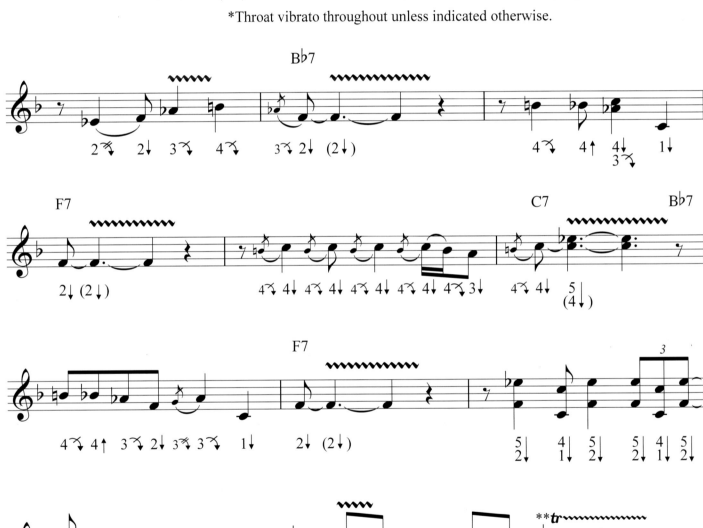

*Throat vibrato throughout unless indicated otherwise.

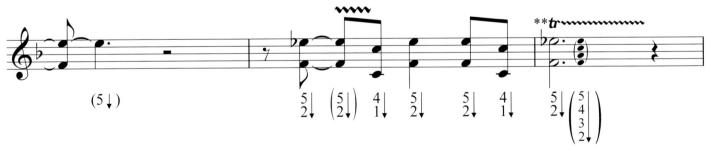

**Tongue blocking trill.

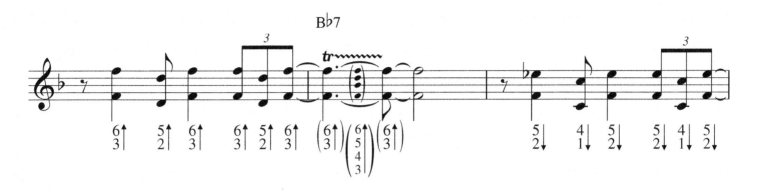

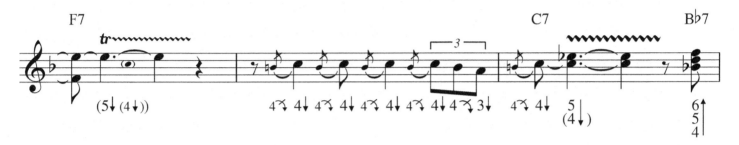

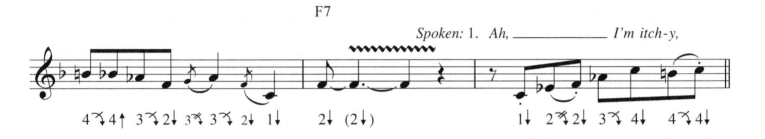

Verse

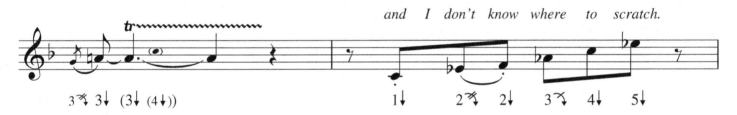

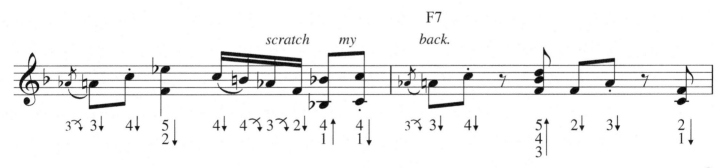

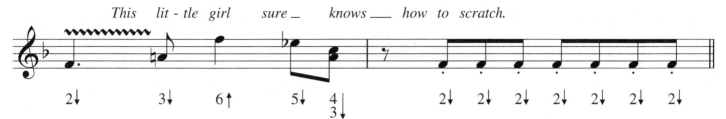

Verse

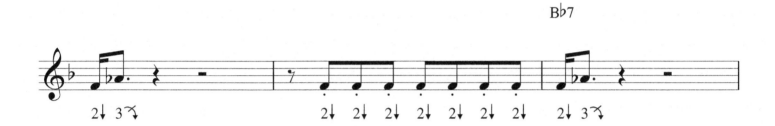

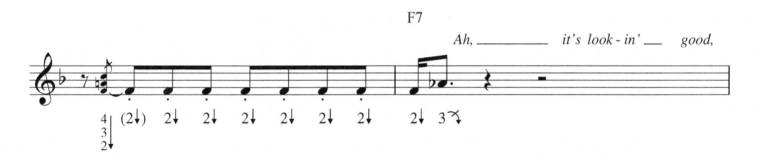

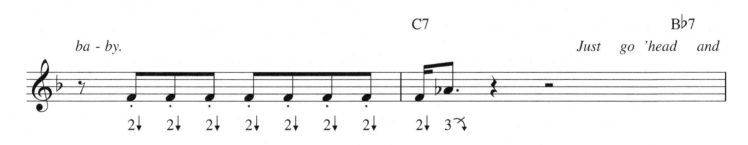

Outro-Harmonica Solo

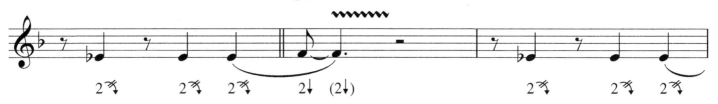

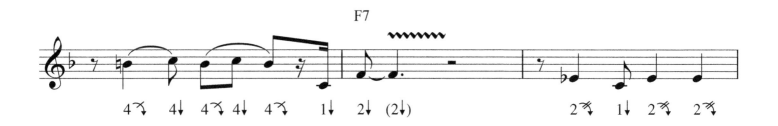

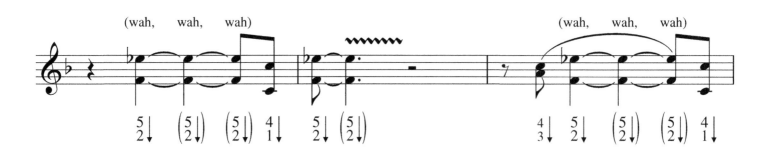

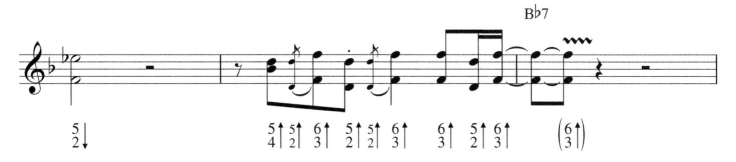

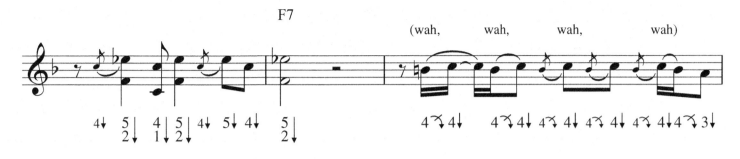

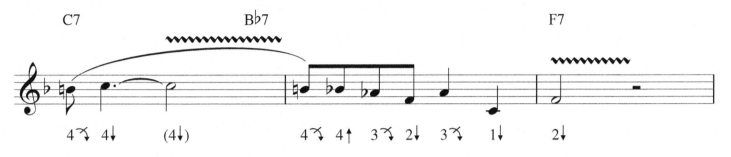

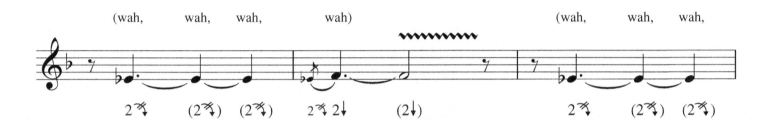

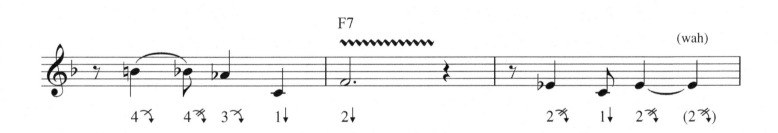

Eyesight to the Blind

Words and Music by Sonny Boy Williamson

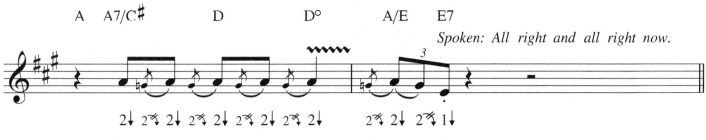

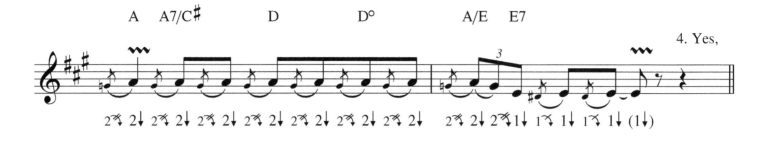

Verse

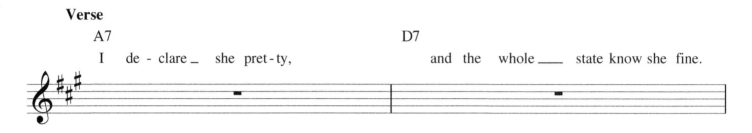

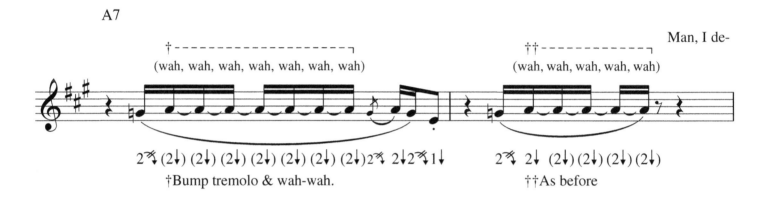

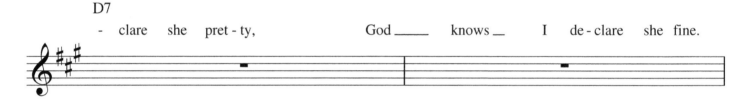

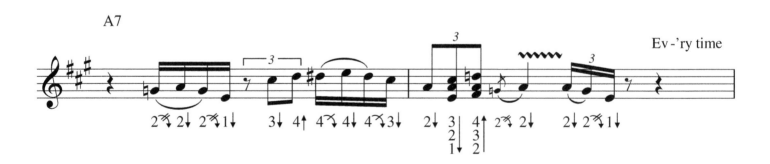

Good Morning Little Schoolgirl

Words and Music by Willie Williamson

H A R M O N I C A
Player: Sonny Boy Williamson I
Harp Key: E Diatonic

*Throat vibrato throughout.

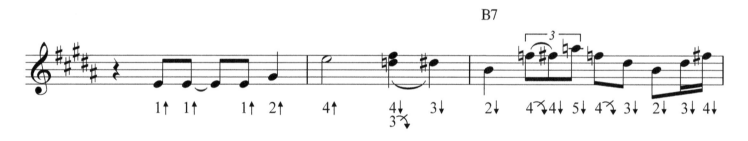

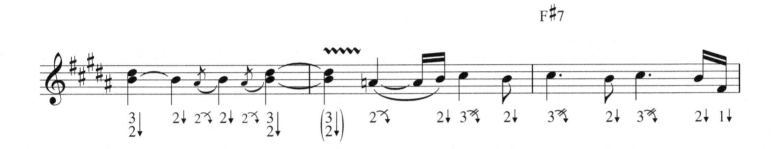

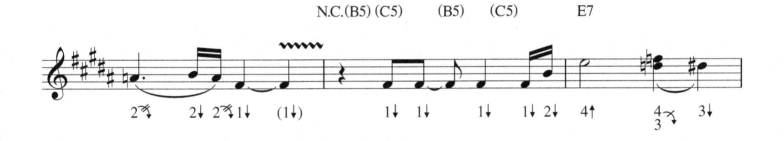

Verse

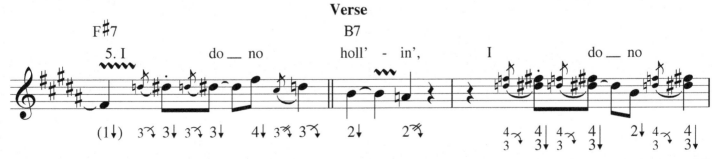

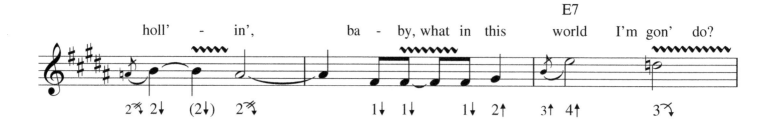

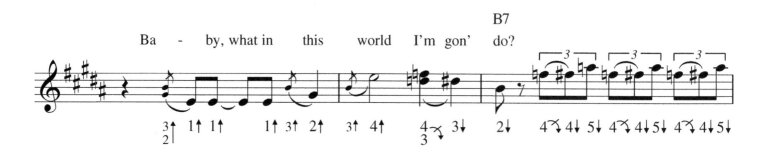

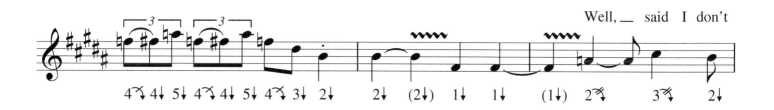

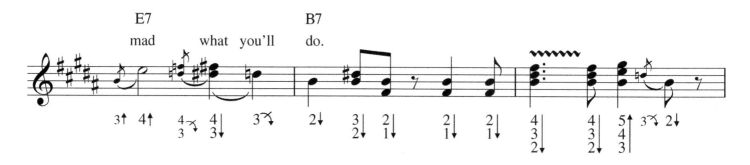

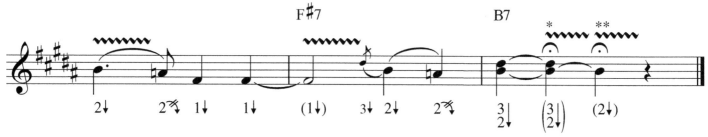

*Tremolo (modulate air flow w/ tongue)

**Throat vibrato

Honest I Do

Words and Music by Jimmy Reed and Ewart G. Abner, Jr.

H A R M O N I C A
Player: Jimmy Reed
Harp Key: A♭ Diatonic

*Hand vibrato throughout.

**Grad. release

I'm Your Hoochie Coochie Man

Written by Willie Dixon

H A R M O N I C A

Player: Little Walter Jacobs
Harp Key: A Diatonic

*Tongue blocking trill.

My Babe

Written by Willie Dixon

HARMONICA
Player: Little Walter
Harp Key: B♭ Diatonic

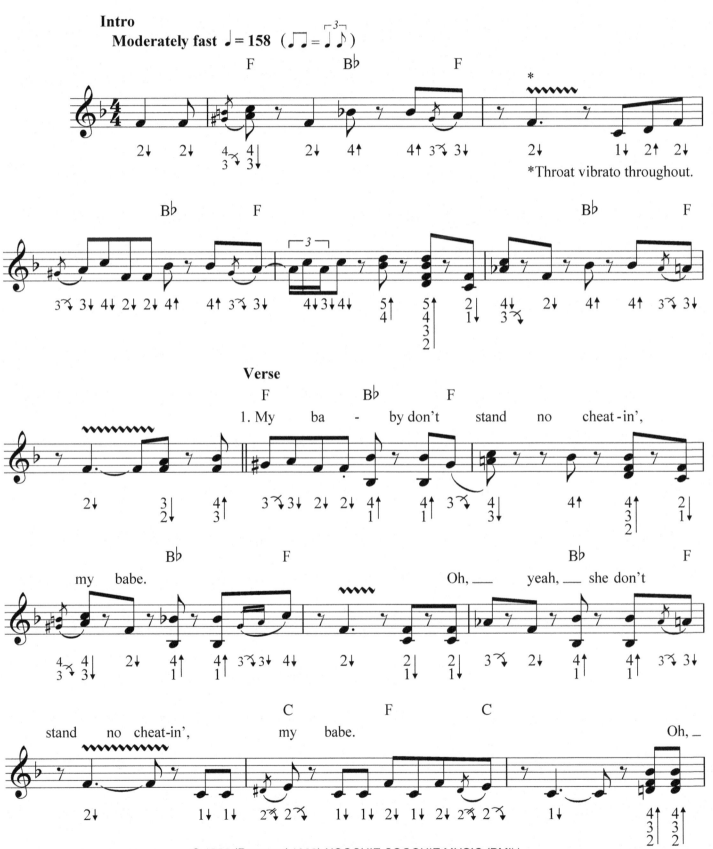

*Throat vibrato throughout.

Harmonica Solo

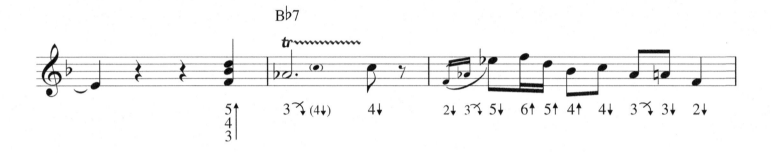

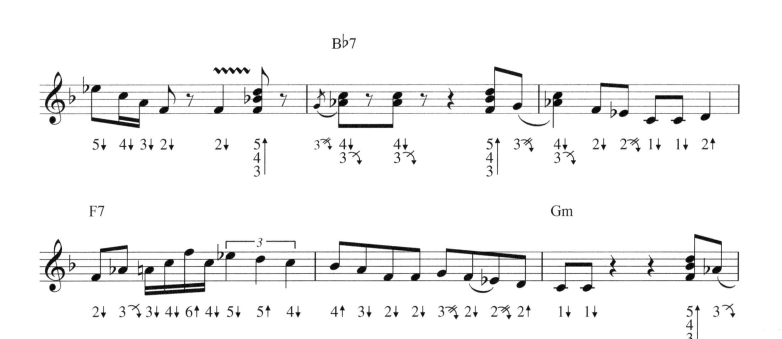

Verse

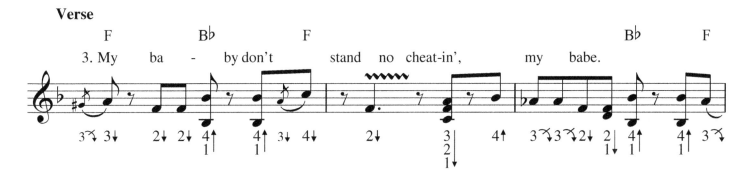

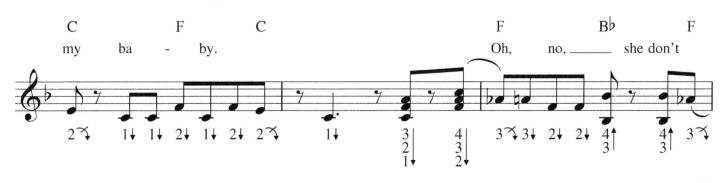

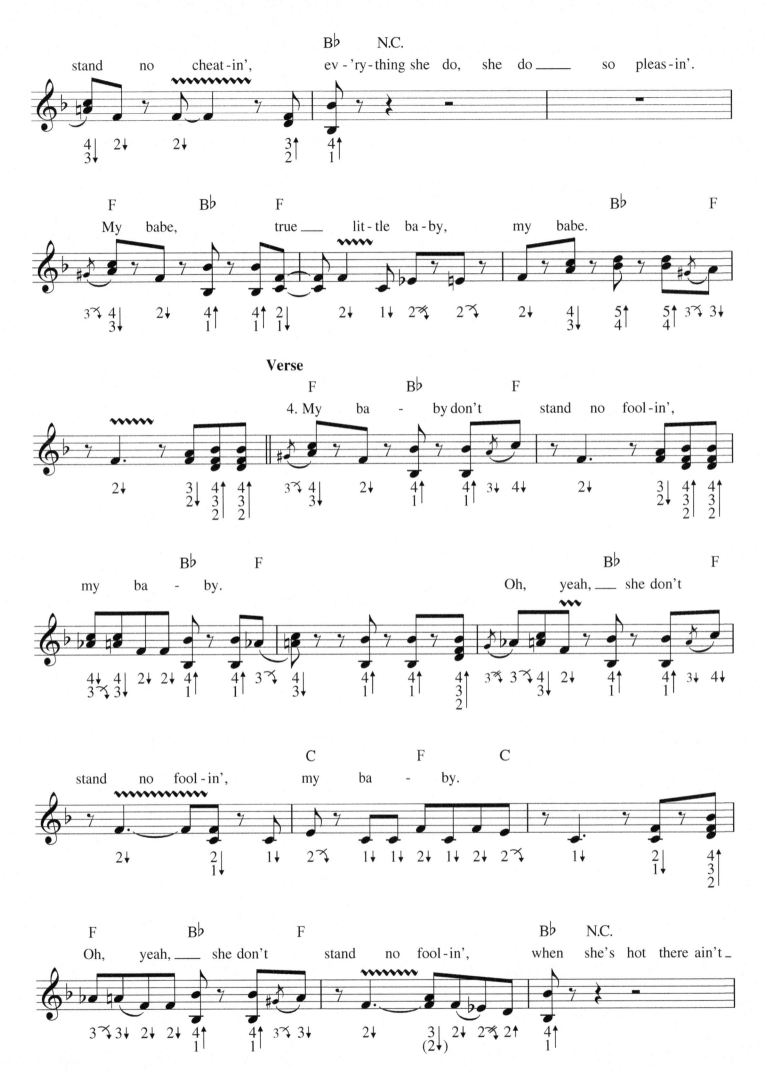

Ride and Roll

Words and Music by Brownie McGhee and Sonny Terry

HARMONICA

Player: Sonny Terry
Harp Key: B Diatonic

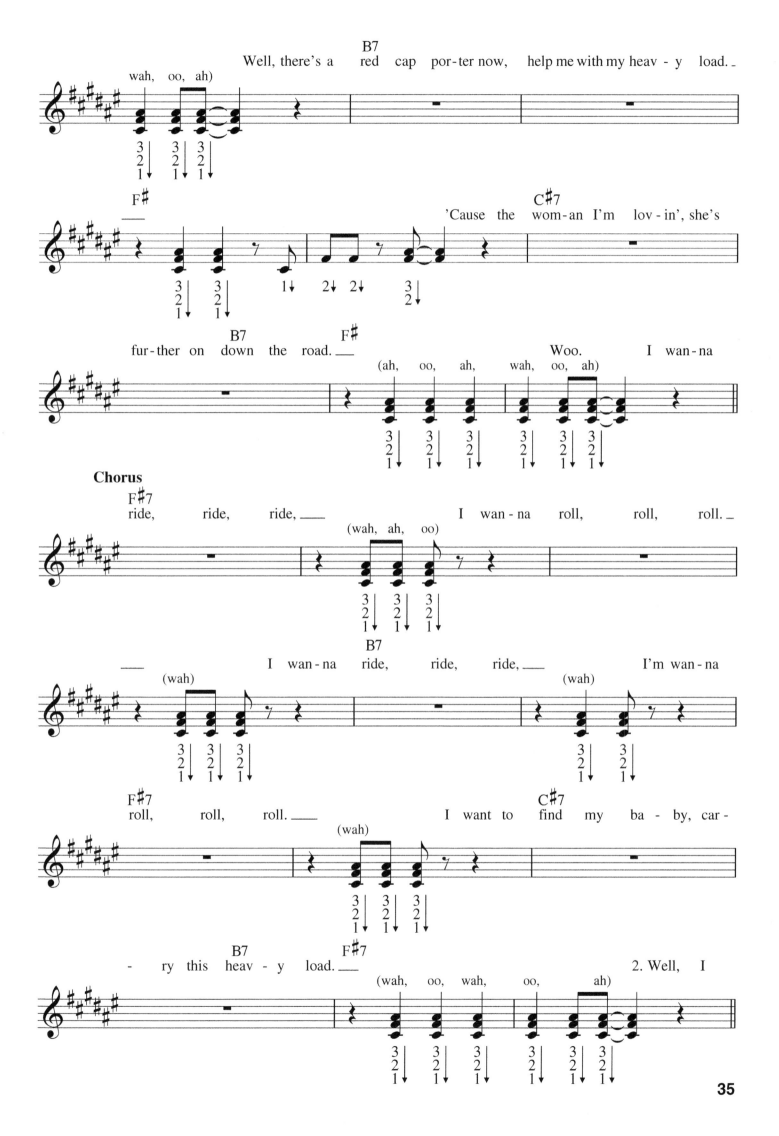

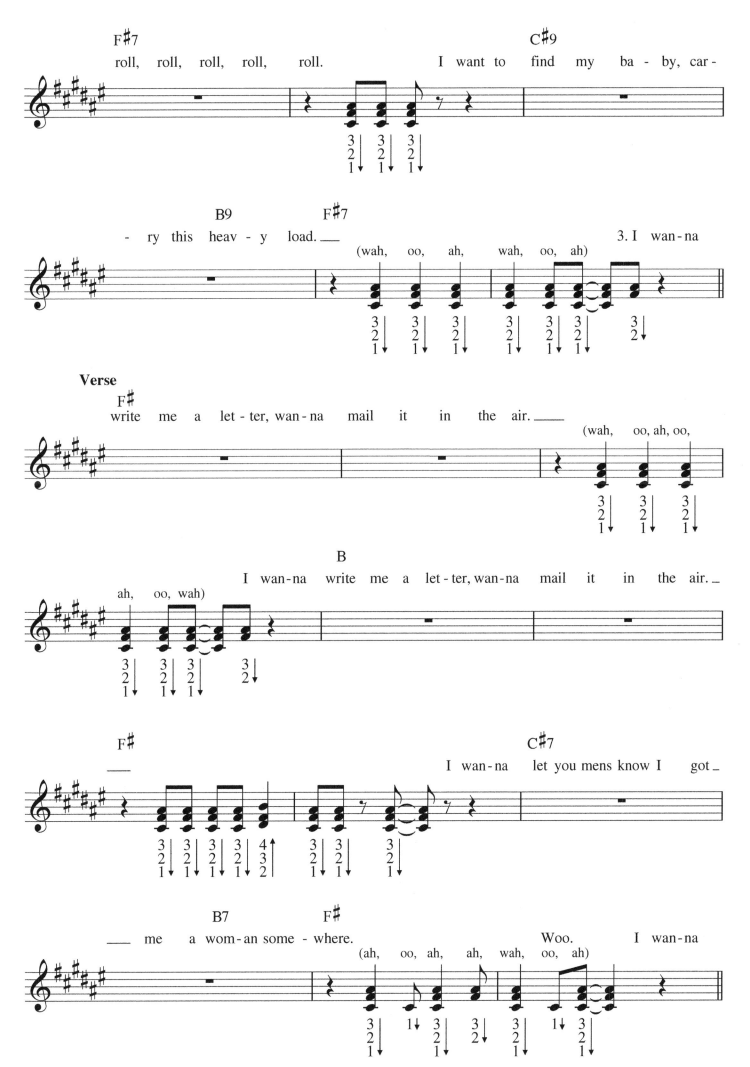

Chorus

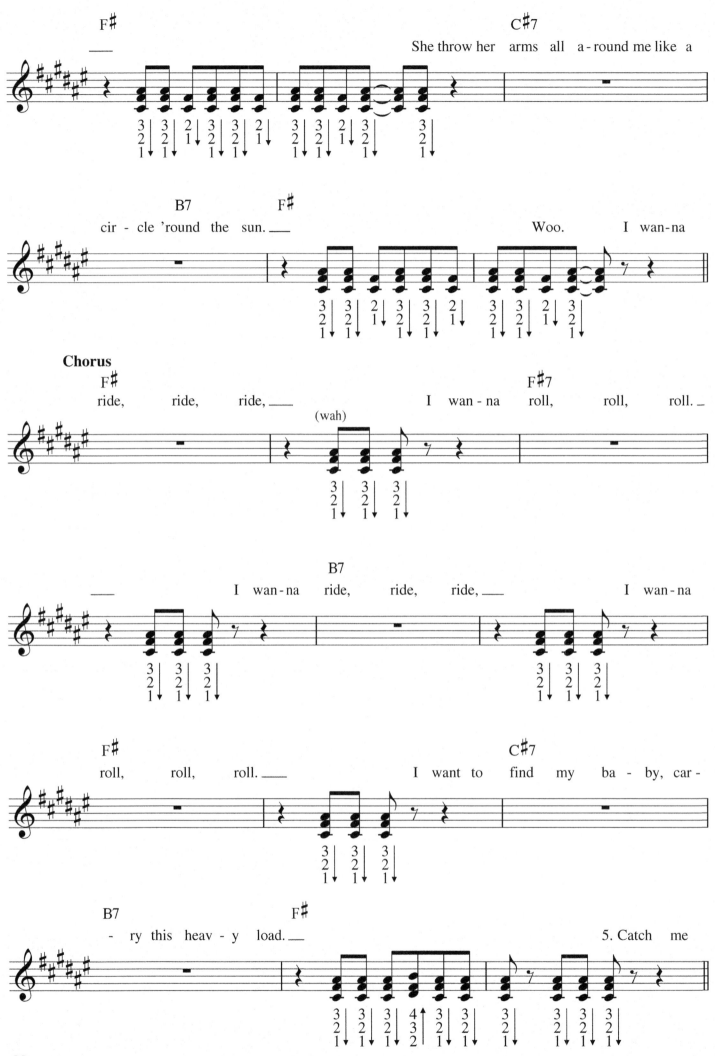

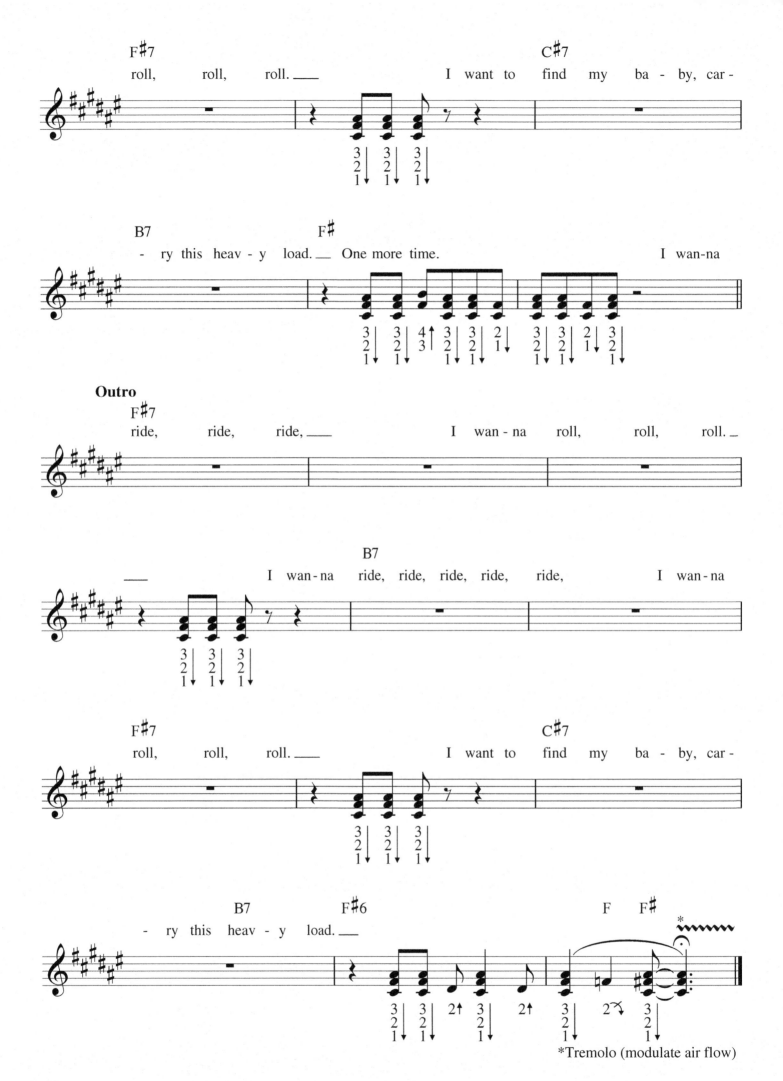

*Tremolo (modulate air flow)

Sweet Home Chicago

Words and Music by Robert Johnson

HARMONICA

Player: Junior Parker
Harp Key: A Diatonic

Harmonica Solo

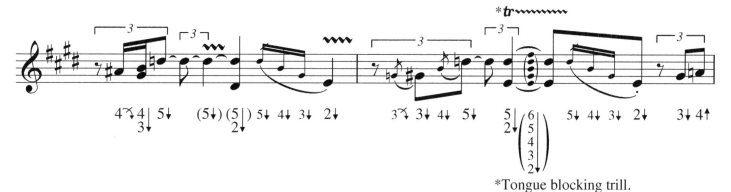

*Tongue blocking trill.

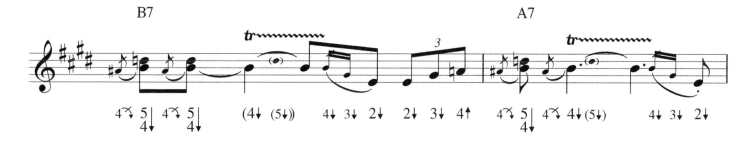

Verse

E7

3. Two and one is three,   three and three is six,

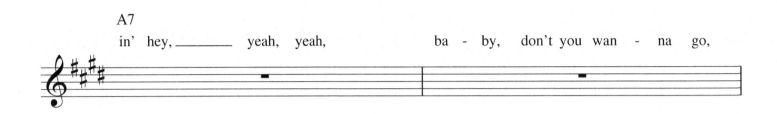

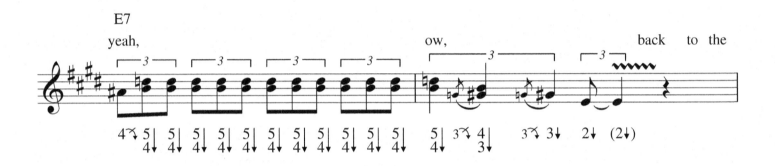

Outro-Tag

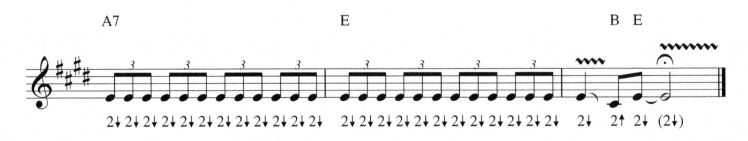

HARMONICA NOTATION LEGEND

Harmonica music can be notated two different ways: on a *musical staff*, and in *tablature*.

THE MUSICAL STAFF shows pitches and rhythms and is divided by bar lines into measures. Pitches are named after the first seven letters of the alphabet.

TABLATURE graphically represents the harmonica music. Each note will be accompanied by a number, 1 through 10, indicating what hole you are to play. The arrow that follows indicates whether to blow or draw. (All examples are shown using a C diatonic harmonica.)

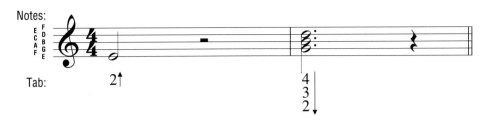

Blow (exhale) into 2nd hole.

Draw (inhale) 2nd, 3rd, & 4th holes together.

Notes on the C Harmonica

Exhaled (Blown) Notes

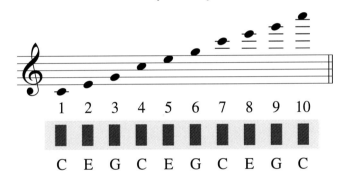

Inhaled (Drawn) Notes

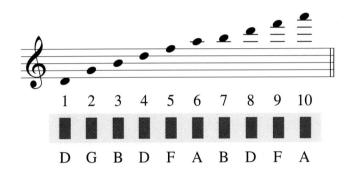

Bends

Blow Bends

• 1/4 step

• 1/2 step

• 1 step

• 1 1/2 steps

Draw Bends

• 1/4 step

• 1/2 step

• 1 step

• 1 1/2 steps

Definitions for Special Harmonica Notation

SLURRED BEND: Play (draw) 3rd hole, then bend the note down one whole step.

GRACE NOTE BEND: Starting with a pre-bent note, immediately release bend to the target note.

VIBRATO: Begin adding vibrato to the sustained note on beat 3.

TONGUE BLOCKING: Using your tongue to block holes 2 & 3, play octaves on holes 1 & 4.

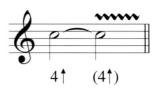

TRILL: Shake the harmonica rapidly to alternate between notes.

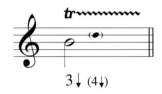

NOTE: Tablature numbers in parentheses are used when:
- The note is sustained, but a new articulation begins (such as vibrato), or
- The quantity of notes being sustained changes, or
- A change in dynamics (volume) occurs.
- It's the alternate note in a trill.

Additional Musical Definitions

D.S. al Coda
- Go back to the sign (%), then play until the measure marked *"To Coda,"* then skip to the section labelled "**Coda**."

 *(accent)*
- Accentuate the note (play initial attack louder).

D.C. al Fine
- Go back to the beginning of the song and play until the measure marked *"Fine"* (end).

(staccato)
- Play the note short.

- Repeat measures between signs.

| 1. | 2. |
- When a repeated section has different endings, play the first ending only the first time and the second ending only the second time.

Dynamics

_p_ • Piano (soft)

 *(crescendo)* • Gradually louder

_mp_ • Mezzo Piano (medium soft)

(decrescendo) • Gradually softer

_mf_ • Mezzo Forte (medium loud)

_f_ • Forte (loud)